W9-ADW-524

World Cities Series

Edited by
Professor R. J. Johnston and Professor P. Knox

Published titles in the series:

Mexico City *Peter Ward*
Lagos *Margaret Peil*
Tokyo *Roman Cybriwsky*
Budapest *György Enyedi and Viktória Szirmai*
Hong Kong *C. P. Lo*
Dublin *Andrew MacLaran*
Vienna *Elisabeth Lichtenberger*
Birmingham *Gordon E. Cherry*
Taipei *Roger M. Selya*
Rome *John Agnew*
Beijing *Victor F. S. Sit*
Glasgow *Michael Pacione*
Harare *Carole Rakodi*
Buenos Aires *David J. Keeling*
Seoul *Joochul Kim and Sang-Chuel Choe*

Forthcoming titles in the series:

Brussels *Alexander B. Murphy*
Havana *Roberto Segre, Mario Coyula and Joseph L. Scarpaci,*
Johannesburg *Keith Beavon*
Lisbon *Jorge Gaspar and Allan Williams*
London *Michael Hebbert*
Montreal *Annick Germain and Damaris Rose*
New York City *David A. Johnson*
Paris *Daniel Noin and Paul White*
Randstad, Holland *Frans M. Dieleman and Jan van Weesep*
Singapore *Martin Perry, Lily Kong and Brenda Yeoh*
Los Angeles *Roger Keil and Don Parsons*
St Petersburg *James H. Bater*

Other titles are in preparation

Seoul